Landscapes of
PAXOS

a countryside guide

Noel Rochford

SUNFLOWER
BOOKS

Dedicated to CV Travel

First published 1990 by
Sunflower Books
12 Kendrick Mews
London SW7 3HG, UK

ISBN 0-948513-40-3

Olive press

Important notes for the reader ⸻

This book could not have been written without the invaluable help I received from CV Travel, who sponsored my visit to Paxos. During my time on the island I stayed at their Villa Marika, shown on page 43. CV Travel, also known as Corfu Villas, is now in its 19th year of providing specialist holiday arrangements all over the Mediterranean, and they offer a very wide range of villa accommodation. For information and brochures, contact CV Travel, 43 Cadogan Street, London SW3 2PR, Telephone 01–581 0851. Their Paxos office is Gaios Travel, Gaios 49082, Paxos.

I have tried to ensure that the descriptions and maps in this book are error-free at press date. The book will be updated, where necessary, whenever future printings permit. It will be very helpful for me to receive your comments (sent in care of the publishers, please) for the updating of future printings. I also rely on those who use this book — especially walkers — to take along a good supply of common sense when they explore. Conditions change fairly rapidly on Paxos, and **storm damage or bulldozing may make a route unsafe at any time.** If the route is not as I outline it here, and your way ahead is not secure, return to the point of departure. **Never attempt to complete a tour or walk under hazardous conditions!** Please read carefully the notes on pages 22 to 26, as well as the introductory comments at the beginning of each walk. Explore **safely**, while at the same time respecting the beauty of the countryside.

Photographs by the author
Map by John Theasby and Pat Underwood
Drawings by Sharon Rochford
Printed and bound in Belgium by Proost

❀ Contents

3

 Preface

Paxos, just 19 sq km of cosy countryside, is little more than a broken fragment of hills sitting anchored off the southern end of Corfu. The hills of Paxos are cloaked in a cool mantle of olive trees. Dark groves of cypresses pierce this silvery-green mantle. In the shade of these wooded hills lie sprinklings of rustic hamlets. But the real beauty of Paxos is the dazzling necklace of turquoise-green coves that collar the eastern coastline.

The moment you step foot on this island you can feel that your stay here is going to be both peaceful and restful. The sleepy fishing villages and the timeless countryside have cast their spell upon you.

You begin to notice just how small the island is, when you keep bumping into the same people on your daily jaunts. This creates a certain friendliness amongst the tourists themselves — a friendliness is further enhanced by the warmth of the islanders. It was this 'neighbourhood' atmosphere that outshone, for me, all the other pleasures of my time on the island.

On Paxos everything is accessible — either a few minutes by public transport, or an hour (never more) on foot. Outside of July and August, when there is little traffic on

the island and a freshness in the air, the charm of the countryside draws you out into it — usually on foot. Everyone seems to go out for a stroll.

Here's where *Landscapes of Paxos* will come in handy. There are a number of well-known beauty spots to be seen, and this book leads you to them ... and to other, more hidden corners that most visitors miss.

Being just that little bit out of the way, Paxos up until now has remained free of those obscene multi-storied apartment buildings and hotels that so badly scar the face of many tourist centres. In fact there is only one hotel on the island at present. But *do remember* that during July and August Paxos does become more like an over-crowded sardine can. Most of the visitors, fortunately, are only day-trippers from Corfu ... we have the mornings and evenings to ourselves.

Happy holiday.

Acknowledgements

A very special thanks to CV Travel (see 'Important notes' on page 2), and to David and Amanda, the company's representatives, who always braved my bombardment of questions with a smile. Also to Richard Coward, who laid the foundations for this book with his booklet, *Footpaths on Paxos*, and his wife Audrey, for their suggestions, information and maps. A final thanks to my sister, Sharon, for her splendid drawings, and to my parents and publisher, who are always so supportive.

Loggos — as perfect as a picture-postcard

Recommended books

Huxley, A and Taylor, W: *Flowers of Greece*. London, Chatto & Windus.

Poulin, O and Huxley, A: *Flowers of the Mediterranean*. London, Chatto & Windus.

Sfikis, G: *Wild Flowers of Greece; Trees and Shrubs of Greece; Medicinal Plants of Greece*. Athens, Efstathiadis.

Drawings of island flora

Acanthus spinosus 21; Agave americana 51; Amaryllis belladonna 37; Anacamptis pyramidalis 53; Anemone 53; Cercis siliquastrum 21; Cyclamen 39; Cupressus sempervirens 41; Erica arborea 52; Euphorbia dendroides 39; Juniperus oxycedrus 39; Nicotiana glauca 11; Phlomis fructicosa 11; Pistacia lentiscus 11; Punica granata 11; Ranunculus 53; Sarcopoterium spinosus 11; Senecio 39; Sternbergia 21, 50; Urginea maritima 53; Vitex agnus-castus 39

Gaios town plan — Key

1 Doctor	9 Town hall
2 Dentist	10 Olive press
3 Bakery	11 Principal car ferry dock
4 Telephones	12 Gaios Travel (tickets for ferries, etc)
5 Post office	13 Caiques (to Moggonissi, etc)
6 Bank	14 Secondary ferry dock
7 Taxi rank	15 Main square
8 Police	⇐⦸ start of Walk 3

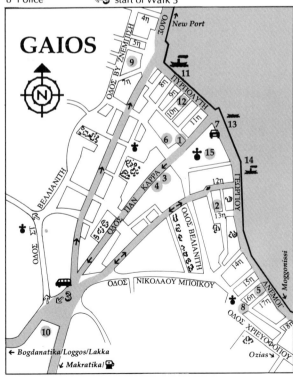

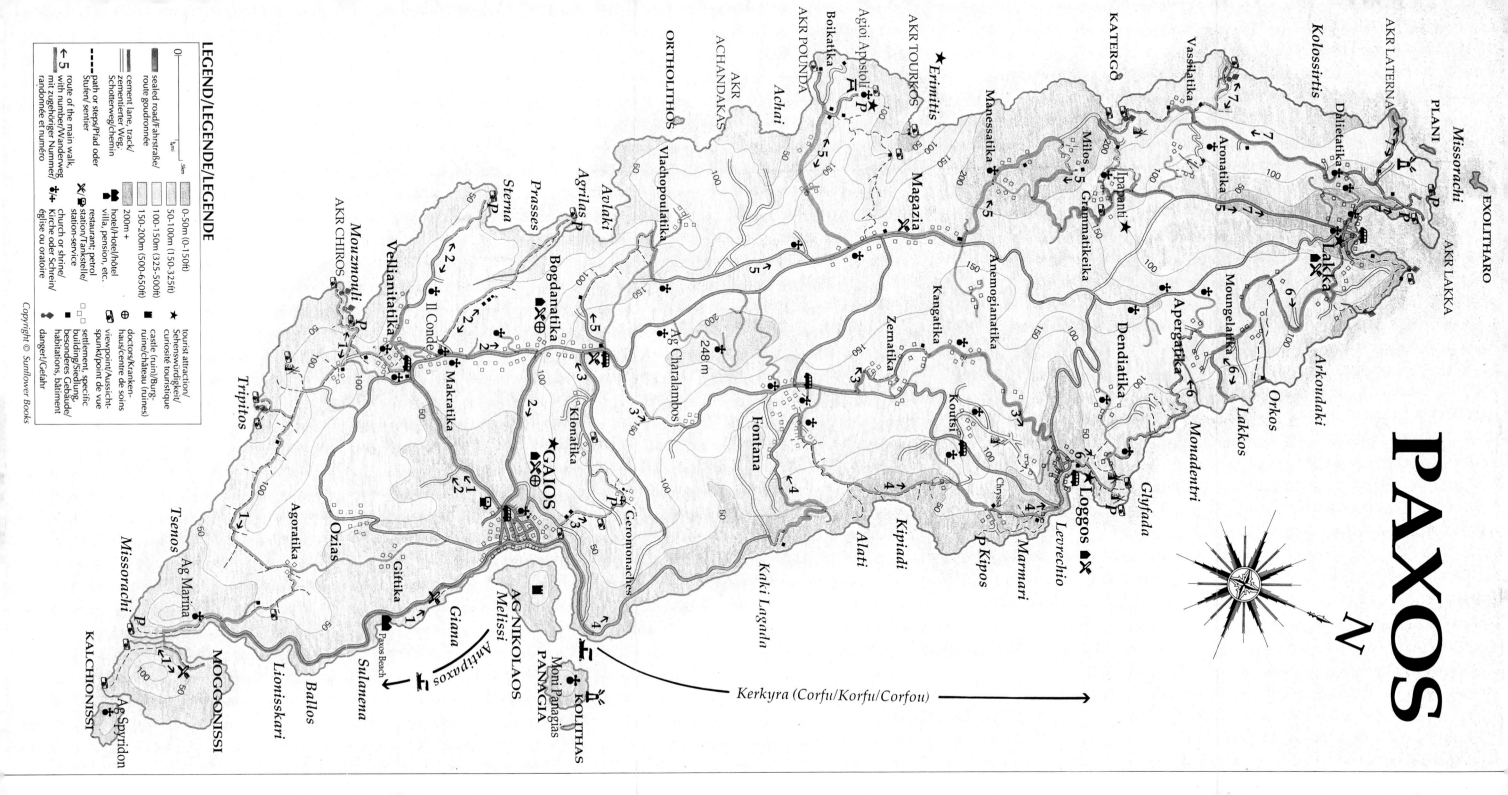

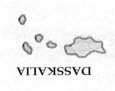

Getting about

Paxos is so small (19 square kilometres) that one can get around quite easily using the fairly regular **bus service**. If you are staying at one of the many secluded tourist villas, and you have children with you, then a hired **car** is advisable. Cars can only be hired from Corfu; this is best arranged before you go to Paxos. **Mopeds** and **motorbikes** are available for hire on Paxos itself. And there's also the appealing option of hiring an outboard **motorboat**, to reach the many otherwise inaccessible coves and beaches that dot the shoreline. Finally you have the option of hiring a **taxi**, and the prices are very reasonable. Check the price before setting out, however, and don't be afraid to bargain politely, if you think you're being taken for a ride metaphorically. Most people, however, get about simply by **strolling**. And what better place for it?

BUS TIMETABLE*

Gaios	Loggos	Lakka	Lakka	Loggos	Gaios
10.00	10.25	10.35	06.30	06.40	07.05
11.00	11.25	11.35	10.30	a	11.00
13.30	13.55	14.05	11.30	11.40	12.05
17.30	17.55	18.05	14.00	a	14.30
			18.30	18.40	19.05

a: Not via Loggos. Buses run daily *except* Sundays and holidays.

FERRY TIMETABLE (PAXOS—CORFU)*

Day	Depart Paxos	Depart Corfu
Mon	07.00 from Lakka direct [1]	09.00 to Gaios direct [1]
	07.30 from Gaios via Lakka [2]	14.00 to Gaios via Lakka [1]
	11.00 from Gaios direct [1]	16.30 to Gaios direct [2]
Tue	07.00 from Gaios direct [1]	08.45 to Gaios direct [1]
	07.30 from Gaios via Mourtos [2]	14.30 to Gaios direct [2]
	08.30 from Gaios direct [3]	16.00 to Gaios direct [3]
	10.30 from Gaios via Loggos [1]	16.30 to Gaios via Loggos [1]
Wed	07.30 from Gaios direct [2]	14.00 to Gaios via Mourtos [2]
	07.45 from Gaios direct [1]	14.45 to Gaios direct [1]
Thur	07.00 from Lakka direct [1]	09.00 to Gaios via Lakka [1]
	07.30 from Gaios via Mourtos [2]	14.00 to Gaios direct [1]
	11.00 from Gaios direct [1]	14.30 to Gaios direct [2]
Fri	07.00 from Gaios direct [1]	14.30 to Gaios direct [2]
	07.30 from Gaios direct [2]	15.00 to Gaios direct [1]
Sat	07.00 from Gaios direct [1]	14.00 to Gaios direct [1]
	07.30 from Gaios direct [2]	14.00 to Gaios via Mourtos [2]
Sun	07.00 from Gaios direct [1]	09.00 to Gaios direct [1]
	17.00 from Gaios direct [1]	19.00 to Gaios direct [1]

* Valid at press date; *recheck* when you arrive on Paxos. **NB: Mourtos is on the mainland**
1 'Pegasus', a high-speed launch; journey time between the islands about 90 minutes
2 'Kamelia', a ferry (maximum 6 cars); journey time 3 hours (3h30min if via Lakka/Mourtos)
3 'Anna Maria', a lovely old passenger ferry; journey time as 'Kamelia'

✿ Picnicking

Who needs an excuse for picnicking on this island, when there are so many out-of-the-way coves to explore? All of them offer ideal swimming conditions and all the solitude you could possibly ask for, in addition to a sylvan backdrop which provides the much-needed shade on a hot day.

There's only one picnic spot amongst the suggestions that follow where you will find tables and benches — Picnic 5 at Ag Apostoli. The rest of the settings I recommend are natural, untouched beauty spots. Some are at exhilarating viewpoints, others are in rustic countryside surroundings, but most of them are at beaches, since that's where you're likely to be heading....

Note that picnic numbers correspond to walk numbers: the location of the picnic spot is shown on the map, where the symbol *P* has been placed on the walking route. Note also that the walking times indicated below are a bit more generous than the times given for ramblers.

1a MOGGONISSI INLET (Photograph opposite)

🚗 by car: 10-15 minutes on foot; park at the end of the Moggonissi road.
🚌 by bus: not easily accessible
From the end of the road, follow the path shown on the facing page. It leads round to the causeway of rocks and over to the taverna and beach. But don't cross the causeway; instead, keep along the shoreline and climb the western sea-cliffs, to sit on the magnificent limestone shelves that create an amphitheatre in the face of the cliff. No shade.

1b MOUZMOULI BAY OVERLOOK (Photograph page 17)

🚗 by car: 10-15 minutes on foot; park by the church in Vellianitatika.
🚌 by bus: 15-20 minutes on foot; alight at the taverna just above the Ozias turn-off.
If you're travelling by bus, use the notes for Walk 1 (page 26) to reach this lookout. If you go by car, from Vellianitatika head behind the church and down past the campanile, where you meet a junction. Turn right and then refer to the second paragraph on page 27: 'Once through the houses ...'. This is a very impressive viewpoint, with shade nearby.

2a STERNA BAY OVERLOOK (Photograph page 32)

🚗 by car: 15-20 minutes on foot; park by the church in Vellianitatika.
🚌 by bus: 20-25 minutes on foot; alight at the taverna just above the Ozias turn-off.
If travelling by bus, follow the notes for Walk 2 to reach this stupendous viewpoint straight across the bay. By car, refer to paragraph 1, page 33: 'Continue past the church....' Shade of trees nearby.

8

2b AGRILAS BEACH (see photograph page 32)

🚗 by car: 20-25 minutes on foot; park off the side of the road at Makratika.

🚌 by bus: 20-25 minutes on foot; alight at Makratika.

Following the notes in the first paragraph on page 34, set out from the church (Il Conde/Pantocratoras, with its noteworthy campanile) in Makratika to descend to Agrilas Beach. Swimming in the inlet is safe, but there is no shade.

On route to Picnic 1a, we leave the car at the end of the Moggonissi road, near the shell of the 6th-century church of Ag Marina, and follow the limestone path heading round to the causeway of rocks.

The islands of Panagia and St Nicholas, from the hills behind Gaios

3 GEROMONACHES (Photograph page 38)

🚗 by car: 10-15 minutes on foot; park at the entrance to the track that turns off into Klonatika — the first track off to your right, as you are descending northeast from Bogdanatika towards the New Port road.
🚌 by bus: 15-20 minutes on foot; alight at Bogdanatika, at the New Port road junction.

Follow the route for Walk 3 as shown on the map; this is very straightforward. Take the first track turning off to the right along the New Port road (motorists park here); then, four minutes later, branch off left into an alleyway that descends to the derelict hamlet of Geromonaches, one of my favourite settings on Paxos — cool, shady, and timeless.

4 KIPOS BEACH

🚗 by car: 5-10 minutes on foot; park above Kipos Beach — see notes below.
🚌 by bus: 15-20 minutes on foot; alight at the Koutsi turn-off.

To get there by car or on foot: Approaching from Loggos, take the cement lane turning off left some 100 metres (yards) above the Koutsi turn-off. (Several signposts for villas mark the entrance to the lane.) Remain along the lane, through a junction and over a crest; then bear right at the fork near the end of the lane, above the beach. This is a very pleasant, secluded spot, and there is shade from olive trees.

5 AGIOI APOSTOLI (photographs pages 22 and 45)

🚗 by car: up to 5 minutes on foot; park at the end of the lane to Ag Apostoli. Turn off in Magazia; the way is well signposted.
🚌 by bus: not recommended; there is no suitable return bus.

This is an excellent setting in the shade of cypress trees, with a picnic table and benches. From the churchyard balcony, you have a splendid view of the Erimitis Cliffs bursting up out of the sea.

6 ABOVE LOGGOS (Photograph page 49)

🚗 by car: 20-25 minutes on foot; park in Loggos.
🚌 by bus: 20-25 minutes on foot; alight in Loggos.

Follow the notes at the start of Walk 6 to explore the promontory above Loggos. A beautiful panorama over the limestone-trimmed coastline lies barely a minute beyond the first mill. Under the shade of olive trees, one could sit all day and admire the seascape. More intimate coves, all offering plenty of shade, can be reached in a further ten minutes (see walk notes), but the descents are steep and not recommended if there are young children in your party.

Pistacia lentiscus

7a CAPE (AKR) LAKKA (Photographs pages 20 and 56)

🚗 by car: 15-20 minutes on foot; park in Lakka.
🚌 by bus: 15-20 minutes on foot; alight in Lakka.

Using the notes for the beginning of Walk 7, picnic anywhere beyond the second beach. From the top of the headland crest you have stunning views embracing the harbour and inland hills shown on page 20. Some shade is on offer. You could also visit the little-frequented beach on the north side of the promontory (photograph page 56), where it is safe to swim, and there is shade from the cliffs.

Phlomis fructicosa
(Jerusalem sage)

7b IPAPANTI CHURCH (Photographs pages 16 and 47)

🚗 by car: up to 5 minutes on foot; park on the lane into Grammatikeika. Coming from Lakka, turn off onto the Manessatika lane. Then take the third lane forking off right (it's less than 1km off the Lakka 'road').
🚌 by bus: not easily accessible.

The (locked) church sits at the end of a path off the lane into the village. You can picnic on the walls below the grand campanile. This is a very peaceful spot, with ample shade.

Punica granata
(Pomegranite)

8 ANTIPAXOS (Photograph page 59)

⛴ by caique: 5-15 minutes on foot

Leave the caique at Vrika and follow the track out. Take the first turn-off to the left (a path, one minute uphill). This path leads down to a lovely small cove called Messovrika. There is no immediate shade on the beach. Most people continue on to Voutoumi Beach — the real beauty spot — so it is likely to be crowded in high season. If you want to follow the crowds, you can get there direct from Messovrika: clamber up the limestone banks at the end of Messovrika and follow a clear path through scrub (there are a couple of short narrow stretches). There's a bar on the hillside above Voutoumi and shade nearby. But it can still be very hot.

Sarcopoterium spinosum
(Thorny burnet)

Nicotiana glauca
(Tobacco shrub)

Country code for walkers and motorists

The experienced rambler is used to following a 'country code' on his walks, but the tourist out for a lark may unwittingly cause damage, harm animals, and even endanger his own life. Please heed this country code.

- **Do not light any fires**. Stub out cigarettes with care.
- **Do not frighten animals.** By making loud noises or trying to touch or photograph them, you may cause them to run in fear and be hurt.
- **Walk quietly** through all hamlets and villages and take care not to provoke any dogs. A walking stick is good protection against a menacing dog, but otherwise, keep it out of sight.
- **Leave all gates just as you find them**. Although you may not see any animals, the gates *do* have a purpose.
- **Protect all wild and cultivated plants.** Don't try to pick wild flowers or uproot saplings. Obviously fruit and other crops are someone's private property and should not be touched. ***Never walk over cultivated land.***
- **Take all your litter away with you.**
- **Walkers — *do not take risks!*** Do not attempt walks beyond your capacity. **Never take a long hike on your own,** and *always* tell a responsible person *exactly* where you are going and what time you plan to return. Remember, if you become lost or injure yourself, it may be a long time before you are found. It's always wise to carry some water, food and a cover-up.

✺ Touring

Paxos is not an ideal island for touring by car — there are no great sights or sites to see and, besides, it's only 9.5km long by 3km wide.

Cars must be rented on Corfu, but this is not expensive. However, unless you consider a car essential for your holiday, I do advise against renting one. Touring can be done on **mopeds** or **motorbikes** and, yes, people of all ages get about this way on the island. Moreover, nearly all the scenic spots on the island are within a short stroll from the **bus** route.

If and when you hire a vehicle, there are important things to remember: always check it out before taking it on the road and report any dents and scratches, etc, lest you find that you get the blame for them. Have you got the necessaries: spare tyre, jack, enough petrol, the telephone numbers of the rental firm (both for office hours and after hours)? Do the lights work? *Read* the rental conditions and the insurance coverage documents.

Important: On Paxos *none* of the mopeds and bikes (or outboard motor boats, for that matter) are insured. You are liable for any damage you incur, and *it is always their estimate.* Be warned, too, that some of the mopeds and

motorbikes are in very poor condition. Drive carefully, as there are a lot of novice riders on the roads, and in July and August getting around can be akin to a Shanghai rush hour. One final word of caution: do note that the island's sole petrol station does sometimes run out of petrol — shipping strikes are the usual cause.

Near Fontana, sooty-faced and -socked sheep graze under the olive trees.

13

AROUND THE ISLAND

Gaios • Moggonissi Island • Gaios • Ozias • Gaios •
Agioi Apostoli Church• Fontana • Loggos • Lakka •
Ipapanti Church • Magazia • Fontana • Gaios

Distance: 35km/22mi; about 2-3 hours' driving

On route: Picnics 1—7 (see pages 8-11); Walks 1—7

*The roads are generally narrow and bumpy, some exceptionally so:
sometimes we follow very small lanes. Passing on these lanes is a
problem. Drive slowly at all times, watching for livestock (and
pedestrians near the villages). During high summer mopeds and motorbikes (and Italian tourists who have come by ferry in their own cars) jam
the roads. Drive with care! There is only one petrol station on the island,
just outside Gaios (hours: 07.30—13.30 and 17.30—20.30, excluding
Sundays and holidays). Avoid the gravel roads in wet conditions.*

Paxos is an island more suited to walking than to
driving. I don't wish to discourage would-be motorists,
but rather to encourage would-be walkers. Of course, if
you have only a day or two, then you will want to see as
much as possible. But here again, many of the beauty spots
on Paxos are only accessible by foot or by sea. Perhaps
that is why the island remains so special.

Under normal conditions, 35km could be covered in
half an hour or so, but this is Paxos … where you will give
the sheep and goats right of way on the tangle of lanes,
stop to admire the beauty spots, and let time take care of
itself.

Before heading to the north of the island from Gaios, we
can do two short 'side' excursions — to Moggonissi Island
and Ozias.

To reach Moggonissi we squeeze past the waterfront
houses (at the southern end of Gaios) and follow the coast.
Pass the bronze statue of Georgis Anemoyiannis, a local
hero who was burnt alive by the Turks during the 1821
Greek Revolution. He was captured after his failed
attempt to set fire to the Turkish fleet.

Our route, a narrow concrete road, runs close to the
seashore for most of the way. Tiny secluded coves lie
ensconced in the limestone-collared coastline. Olive
groves cascade down the gentle inclines to the edge of the
sea. Less than a kilometre out of town, you pass a taverna
(✕) on the left and, shortly after, the rather discreet Paxos
Beach Hotel (▲▲), the only hotel on the island. It sits above
a cove on a hillside, amidst olive trees.

Approaching **Moggonissi** Island (4km ✕) the olive
groves subside and maquis takes over the countryside; the
greenery intensifies. The island sits across a shallow beryl-
green inlet that narrows to a hair's breadth, only *jus*

14

making Moggonissi an island. Through this 'V' one can see Antipaxos rising up out of the sea in the background. Moggonissi's small sandy beach and taverna (photograph page 29) are very popular with those staying in Gaios, and caiques ply frequently between Gaios and the beach.

To reach the beach and taverna follow the limestone path off the end of the road, by the crumbled shell of the

Gaios from the hills above the town. This photograph was taken not far from the track climbed at the start of Walk 3.

6th-century church of Ag Marina (see photograph page 9). A causeway of rocks takes you across the inlet. Take a bit of care — the rocks are slippery, and the water is sometimes ankle-deep. Walk 1 visits Moggonissi, and Picnic 1a is an especially pleasant setting for evening 'dining' in the open air.

Returning to Gaios, we can continue to Ozias. Leaving Gaios on the Makratika road (left at the fork on the outskirts of town), pass the petrol station (⛽) and climb into a small rocky valley stepped with olive groves. Barely a kilometre up you reach the Ozias turn-off (signposted, but obscured by olive trees). Turn left for the hamlet. Colourful roadside gardens enliven the countryside here. Each garden has its complement of citrus, fig and pomegranate trees — and the enormous old ribbed water jars (see title page) which were once used for water storage, but are now only a decorative feature. Walls crippled by old age and derelict buildings sit back amongst the trees. The road meanders through this arcadian countryside, always in the shade of olive trees. In autumn the hillsides are flecked with carmine-coloured cyclamen, and you'll spy pockets of bright yellow *Sternbergia*; spring brings its own floral extravaganza, with deep blue bellflowers, lily-white arums, an assortment of anemones, and violet hyacinths.

Ozias (10km) is a pleasant country village straddling the top of a ridge. Small cottages line the side of the road. This area was the first part of Paxos to be inhabited, and the settlement once spread as far as Vellianitatika. Descending back into Gaios, you may spot a mass of

Ipapanti, the oldest church on Paxos (Walks 5 and 7; Picnic 7b). There's a photograph of the campanile on page 47.

Picnic 1b: the outlook over Mouzmouli Bay, a 10-15 minute walk from the church in Vellianitatika.

rubble from collapsed walls strewn about the slopes.

Now, to begin the 'real' tour, head once again up the Makratika road, soon passing the turn-off to Vellianitatika (Walk 2) on your left. If you were to park by the church in Vellianitatika, you could explore two superb viewpoints: the outlook over Mouzmouli Bay shown above (Picnic 1b), and the equally fine overview of Sterna Bay shown on page 32 (Picnic 2a).

Just beyond the Vellianitatika turn-off, the 18th-century roadside church of El Conde (also called Pantocratoras) in **Makratika** catches your attention with its fine campanile. The church door was made to order — the last Venetian mayor wanted to be able to enter the church on horseback! To enjoy Picnic 2b at Agrilas Beach, you would set off through the archway of the campanile.

The large, drawn-out village of **Bogdanatika** (13km ▲✕⊕; Walk 5) follows. Two more roads from Gaios join us from the right here. (Were you to fork off right along the New Port road, you would reach the setting for Picnic 3 — the enchanting derelict hamlet of Geromonaches, shown on page 38.) As we leave Bogdanatika, we pass the turn-off left to Vlachopoulatika, a picturesque scattering of houses where you could potter around and stretch your legs, using the notes for Walk 5 on page 44.

Climbing the cypress-wooded slopes, we circle below the island's highest point — a hillock 248m/815ft high. The imposing 19th-century belfry of Ag Charalambos on the 'mountain' towers over the roadside. Rising high above the trees, it stands like a sentry post, looking out to the south of the island. We, too, look back to the south — over undulating hills and, beyond them, to Antipaxos.

Descending the 'mountainside' we enter **Magazia** (16km ✕; Walk 5), where we make a side-trip by turning left on a cement lane signposted to Agioi Apostoli. A kilometre down this narrow and bumpy lane, we turn up a track heading off right (between a garage and a house) onto the church driveway. **Agioi Apostoli** ★ (17km 🚶🚗; Walk 5) is a very simple church, but we have really come for the view of the **Erimitis Cliffs** ★ — one of the 'sights' of Paxos. These blaring white limestone cliffs, shown on page 22, plummet hundreds of feet into an aquamarine sea — a spell-binding sight. A table and benches here allow you to picnic in comfort (Picnic 5). Be sure, too, to stretch you legs by strolling from the church down to the superb viewpoint over Achai Bay and its cloistered caves, shown on page 45. Use the map or the notes on page 46 to follow the coastal track to this nearby viewpoint. Ag Apostoli is always kept locked, unfortunately, due to thievery in the past.

Back in Magazia, and just beyond the turn-off to Ag Apostoli, we bear right for Fontana and Loggos. A flock of sooty-faced and -socked sheep graze amidst the trees. When you're out walking here, bells always alert you to their presence. **Fontana**, half a kilometre further along, boasts three *cafeneions* and as many churches. Walk 4 skirts the back of this village, and Walk 3 passes through it. Notice the olive press on the roadside, as you pass by the village (see sketch on page 2). Heaps of olive residue lie across the road from the press. You can't miss the resinous aroma. Paxos has only two modern olive presses, but there are still a number of the old ones about. In your strolls over the island you'll venture upon the remains of derelict presses. The process for making olive oil has remained unchanged. The olives are crushed with stone grinding wheels, and the pulp is then strained by pressing it through a layered sacking-like material, to rid it of lumps and foreign particles. At first the drained oil is dark and cloudy, but eventually it clears. (This unprocessed oil gets poured over our Greek salads and usually gives us indigestion for the first week of our holiday….)

Winding down to Loggos, you pass the turn-off right to Kipos Beach (Picnic 4). On your left, you'll see a ruined windmill below, in a clearing amidst olive trees. Short walk 3-3 passes by this mill, shown opposite. Notice the extraordinary shape of the olive trees on these inclines. They have massive twisted and twirling trunks, and are pitted with 'eyes'. Nearer to the sea, colonnades of cypress trees line the roadside. Soon Levrechio Beach appears through the hillside trees. This white-stone cove is very popular, since it's the closest beach to Loggos.

Rounding a corner, we overlook a tight horseshoe-shaped bay and descend into **Loggos** ★ (22km ▲ ✕; Walks 3, 4, 6; Picnic 6). To me, this village, shown on pages 4-5 and 43, is the most appealing of the three fishing ports on Paxos. The pastel-coloured houses lean up against one another — as houses should in a *real* fishing village. And how's this for authenticity: you have to sidle past the houses and squeeze between the tables and chairs of the two waterfront restaurants to drive out of the village. Where else in the world would you drive straight through a restaurant? It's even more fun when you go through by bus — the diners quickly tuck in their toes! Loggos also seems to have more cats per capita than anywhere else in the world, so drive through it with your foot on the brakes.

The enclosing hills make for good exploring around here. There are some derelict windmills (like the one shown below), tucked-away hamlets, beaches to suit all tastes, and most important of all, peace and quiet — outside of July and August, that is. Climbing out of the deep valley that curves back inland behind Loggos, we meet a junction. Bear right for Lakka, our next port of call. Charming old villas grace the cool, shady olive groves.

Signs of mass tourism are non-existent on Paxos; however, coming into **Lakka** ★ (25km ▲ ✕; Walks 5-7), one can't help but notice a couple of very ominous-looking apartment buildings. These aside, Lakka still remains much more a fishing port than a tourist enclave. Two pincers of land embrace the shallow sandy-bottomed bay here, keeping it sheltered and calm — hence the deluge of sailboats and windsurfers. Somehow they even manage to water-ski amidst the confusion of

Old windmill below Koutsi (Short walk 3-3)

craft. But if it's solitude you're after, you'll find it on Cape (Akr) Lakka, where you can revel in superb landscapes and fine swimming spots. For children, the two beaches on the left side of the bay are ideal. Explore this headland using the notes for Picnic 7a (see photographs below and on page 56).

On our return to Gaios, we take the wide gravel road that disappears into a large valley burrowing into the hills behind Lakka. An unkempt forest of olive trees fills the valley floor. A kilometer along this rough 'road', we turn off to the right onto a cement lane (*not* signposted), to visit **Ipapanti Church ★** in Grammatikeika. Just over half a

Lakka, from the promontory above the port. This is one of the delightful settings for Picnic 7a.

kilometre up this shady country lane, a narrower lane (the third you come to) strikes off right into the village. Again, there are no signposts to alert you, but (at present) a solitary house sits on the roadside opposite your turn-off. *Note: The lane only goes a couple of hundred metres towards the hamlet and then ends; there is only parking space for a couple of cars.* We've come this far to see the church, not because it's an architectural masterpiece, but because it is the oldest on Paxos and atypical: two brothers built the church in 1601; the Ionian baroque bell-tower was added in 1772. And one cannot ignore its fine setting — high up on a densely-wooded hillside deep in the tail of the valley, quite out of touch with the rest of Paxos. This is the setting for Picnic 7b; see photographs on pages 16 and 47.

Heading home, we return to the gravel road and bear right. At the Loggos/Magazia junction keep right again. Ascending back over the island's backbone of hills, you look down into tree-clad valleys that wind their way seaward. You will have noticed that, on Paxos, the rural villages are made up of dispersed scatterings of houses, rather than forming a tight nucleus, as they do on Corfu, for example.

Back in **Magazia**, we turn off once more for Fontana, where we again keep right, and pass through the village (remaining straight on) to take the coastal route back to Gaios. This bumpy stretch of gravel road drops down through a landscape matted in vegetation. We reach the sea at Kaki Lagada Beach (Walk 4) — an ideal spot to finish up our day with a refreshing dip. Winding around the eastern flanks we pass above a couple more delectable coves, before joining the New Port road and descending back into Gaios.

Cercis siliquastrum
(Judas tree)

Sternbergia

Acanthus spinosus

✽ Walking

Paxos is ideal for strolling, a place where you can amble along … oblivious of time and with no particular destination in mind. The countryside is gentle and friendly, the cove-indented coastline irresistible and fun to explore.

All the walks in this book are *graded* with the inexperienced walker in mind.* Moreover, if you can't summon up the energy for a 2- to 3-hour ramble, have a look at the short walks described; they get you to all the island's beauty spots. Still too long a distance on foot? Then try the picnic suggestions — *very* short walks, especially suitable on really hot days.

Experienced ramblers will no doubt find all the walks in this book quite easy.

*Important: In addition to grade, **times** are given (at the start of each walk, and to reach various points). Please note that I am a very fit, very fast walker. **A walk may take you two to three times as long as it takes me** — especially in summer. Compare your pace with mine before doing a long walk, and be sure to take transport connections into account.

Where to stay

Paxos is so small that any part of the island can be reached within half an hour if you have a rented car or moped. The island is also relatively well served by bus and *caique* (to Moggonissi Island and Antipaxos).

The **three main tourist centres** are the ports of Gaios (the capital), Loggos and Lakka. In these places you can find villas, apartments and rooms. The only hotel on the island at present is the Paxos Beach Hotel, one kilometre south of Gaios. Remember that during the high season accommodation is *very* hard to find, if you have not booked it in advance.

Weather

The kindest months for your strolls around Paxos and Antipaxos are on either side of summer: April to June and September to October. July and August, when temperatures can reach 30°C, are the hot and sticky months — but sea breezes do help to keep you cool. This the time for short strolls only — to the beach or a picnic spot.

Spring is announced in April with warmth in the sun and an extravaganza of wild flowers, but the rain isn't over yet. By June a rainy day is considered unlucky, and in July

or August, a phenomenon. Towards the end of September there's a freshness in the air again, with an occasional passing thunderstorm. In early October it's time for a cardigan and, as the month progresses, the cloudy days turn to rainy days. It's not the time for a beach holiday, but the haze-free cerulean sky and lush greenery, where autumn flowers hide, make this an exhilarating time to walk.

Picnic 5 affords this fabulous view over the Erimitis Cliffs.

Nuisances

The only thing one has to watch out for on Paxos is **snakes**. May and June is when the snakes come out to play … and October, to a lesser extent. When walking in long grass, take a stick to beat the grass, and be vigilant around springs and water sources in the hot summer months. **Dogs** in general are no bother; they are all bark and no bite. Threatening them with a stone does the trick. **Scorpions** are nocturnal creatures, and the only time you'll encounter them is when you move logs or rocks. Do so carefully. Their sting is not dangerous, just very painful. **Bees** and **wasps** abound in summer, particularly around water. Approach all water sources and ponds, etc with care. If you are allergic to bee stings, make sure you have the necessary pills with you. Perhaps the biggest nuisance — but only in mid-summer — is the **horse-fly**. Long trousers and long-sleeved shirts lessen the problem. Avoid **ticks** by wearing long socks. Always watch out for **sea urchins** when swimming; they are found close to the shore in many coves and beaches. You'll also encounter, or hear, lots of **hunters**. They blast away at anything that moves or flies. Don't be afraid to shout and let them know that you are in the area….

What to take

I've listed at the heading of each walk the minimum *year-round* equipment, relying on you to modify the list according to the season. Below is a check list of things to pack, if you plan to do a lot of walking.

walking boots or **sturdy shoes**
(whichever you choose,
they must be broken-in
and comfortable)
waterproof rain gear
(outside summer months)
long trousers, tight at the ankles
(sun and tick protection)
long-sleeved shirt (sun protection)
small rucksack
extra pair of (long) socks
plastic groundsheet

bandages and band-aids
plastic plates, cups etc.
protective sun cream
anorak (zip opening)
knives and openers
sunhat, sunglasses
antiseptic cream
insect repellent
cardigans
spare boot laces
whistle
torch

The items highlighted in bold type are mandatory. Please don't ruin your holiday with a sprained ankle or sunstroke. Always carry a sunhat, long-sleeved shirt and long trousers with you, and put them on when you have had enough sun. Take your lunch in a shady spot on hot days, and carry a good supply of fruit and water.

Greek for walkers

In the majority of the tourist areas you hardly need to know any Greek at all, but once you are out in the countryside a few words of the language will be helpful. Anyway, it is nice to be able to communicate, if only a little, and people warm to your attempts.

Here's one way to ask directions in Greek and understand the answers you get! First memorise the few 'key' and 'secondary' questions given below. Then, *always follow up your key question with a second question demanding a yes (ne) or no (ochi) answer.* Greeks invariably raise their heads to say 'no', which looks to us like the beginning of a 'yes'! (By the way, *'ochi'* (no) might be pronounced as **o**-hee, **o**-shee or even **oi**-ee.)

Following are the two most likely situations in which you may need to use some Greek. The dots (...) show where you will fill in the name of your destination. Ask someone who lives on the island to help you with the pronunciation of place names.

■ *Asking the way*

The key questions

English	Approximate Greek pronunciation
Good day, greetings	**Hair**-i-tay
Hello, hi (informal)	**Yas**-sas (plural); **Yia**-soo (singular)
Please —	**Sas** para **kaloh** —
Where is	**pou** ee-**nay**
the road that goes to...?	o **thro**-mo stoh...?
the footpath that goes to...?	ee mono-**pati** stoh...?
the bus stop ?	ee **stassis** ?
Many thanks.	Eff-hah-ree-**stoh** po-li

Secondary question leading to a yes/no answer

English	Approximate Greek pronunciation
Is it here?	**Ee**-nay **etho**?
Is it there?	**Ee**-nay eh-**kee**?
Is it straight ahead?	**Ee**-nay kat-eff-**thia**?
Is it behind?	**Ee**-nay **pee**-so?
Is it to the right?	**Ee**-nay **thex**-ya?
Is it to the left?	**Ee**-nay aris-teh-**rah**?
Is it above?	**Ee**-nay eh-**pano**?
Is it below?	**Ee**-nay **kah**-to?

■ *Asking a taxi driver to take you somewhere and return for you, or asking a taxi driver to collect you*

English	Approximate Greek pronunciation
Please —	**Sas** para **kaloh** —
would you take us to ...?	Tha **pah**-reh mas stoh...?
Come and pick us up	**El**-la na mas **pah**-reh-teh
from ... at ...	apo ... stees ...

(Instead of memorising the hours of the day simply point out on your watch the time you wish to be collected.)

1 GAIOS • VELLIANITATIKA • AKR CHIROS • TRIPITOS ARCH • MOGGONISSI ISLAND • GAIOS

Distance: 9km/5.5mi; 2h30min   **See also photographs pages 9, 17**

Grade: fairly easy, if you exclude the descents both to Akr Chiros and the Tripitos Arch. If you do the whole walk, the grade is moderate to strenuous. The descents to Chiros Point and the Tripitos Arch follow goats' paths, with a possibility of vertigo. They are recommended for more experienced walkers, *and only in dry weather.*

Equipment: sturdy shoes or walking boots, sunhat, suncream, long-sleeved shirt, long trousers, cardigan, rainwear, bathing suit, picnic, water

How to get there: 🚌 to Gaios or the Vellianitatika turn-off
To return: 🚌 from Gaios

Short walks:

1   Follow the entire walk, but exclude the descents to Akr Chiros and the Tripitos Arch: 1h45min. Fairly easy.

2   Gaios—Vellianitatika—Tripitos Arch—Vellianitatika—Gaios: 2h. Moderate to strenuous. Recommended only for experienced walkers; possibility of vertigo. 🚌 to and from Gaios.

T he Tripitos Arch is one of the island's natural wonders. It takes you by surprise: you peer over the sheer sea-cliffs and see not far below you an impressive archway of rock hanging off the island. It requires a bit of a scramble to reach the arch but, if you're sure-footed, don't miss this descent. Otherwise, just enjoy the peace and quiet of the shady mule tracks we follow. Then paddle over to Moggonissi Island and take a dip in the beautiful inlet that lights up this picturesque corner of Paxos.

Start the walk by leaving Gaios on the road that climbs to Makratika: take the street that leaves the main square (the *platia*). When it forks, a minute out, keep left. This bumpy country road ascends steadily into the spine of modest hills that runs down the centre of the island. Twisted old olive trees lean out over the road. Paxos seems to be one extended canopy of olive groves — they cover most of the island and have done so since the Venetian era. It's estimated that the island supports some 300,000 of them. It is said that a well-nurtured tree is able to produce up to 20 kilos of olive oil in a good year.

Crumbled stone walls terrace the rocky limestone hillsides. Around **10min** uphill, you pass the Ozias turn-off. Barely a minute beyond it, reach a bar/restaurant on the left, off a curve. Leave the road here and follow the path that heads behind the restaurant, passing a church on your left. Then, just before you would join the Ozias road (it lies some two minutes below), swing right uphill on a mule track. This wide cobbled trail climbs to

Vellianitatika; a high stone wall lines the right-hand side of the route, and terracing litters the slope.

Come to a junction below the village *platia* (where there is a church) and veer left immediately. Once through the houses, curve left on a dirt path. Circling a solitary house with a garden on our left, we come to a junction and turn right along a driveway. Then we branch off the drive onto the first path heading off to the right. Stone walls hem

Tripitos Arch

us in. When the next junction (which looks more like a square) brings you to a halt, head to the right, towards the coast. Ignore the narrow alleyways leading off the path.

Less than ten minutes from Vellianitatika we're at the very edge of the cliffs rising above Mouzmouli Bay. This gaping bite out of the coastline, shown on page 17, is the setting for Picnic 1b. Approach the cliffs with care. To reach the left arm of the bay — Chiros Point — and to enjoy a precarious view of some sea caves, continue up around the top of the cliffs to the left. A minute up, a path swings off left between stone walls. Here we descend to the point. The safest route is through a gap in the stone wall that follows the side of the cliff. This gap is on the right, six metres (yards) inside the path that forks off to the left. (Via the cliff-tops the way is vertiginous and dangerous.) Once inside the enclosing walls, follow the seaward wall for two minutes — or until you see another gap that lets you out through the lower wall, where you again rejoin the path.

Then wind your way down the steep and rocky, maquis-clad slope, perhaps at times passing a little *too* close to the edge for comfort. Just over five minutes down, where you're on the arm that encloses the bay, peer *very carefully* over the top of the cliff to see three well-hidden sea caves to your right. Minutes further along, reach a cement geographical peg, from where you have a fine view back into the bay and to the island of Antipaxos in the south. *Walk with care and attention along this stretch of the route.*

To continue the walk, we return to the square-like junction, three minutes beyond the Mouzmouli Bay viewpoint, and this time we head along the alley to our right. Leave it alongside an olive press, to take a cement lane which ends metres (yards) further uphill. A garden flooded with colour sits at the end of the lane. Follow the paved path that heads along the right-hand side of the garden. At

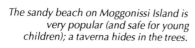

The sandy beach on Moggonissi Island is very popular (and safe for young children); a taverna hides in the trees.

the fork some metres (yards) along, turn off to the right, then keep straight on (ignoring a branch-off to the right). You pass through a friendly cluster of houses buried amidst the olive groves high on the hillside. Tired stone walls age the face of the countryside like wrinkles.

Minutes along, we descend onto an old track. A minute uphill, to the right, it ends. Three alleyways lead off it. (Note: Two minutes up the alley on your immediate right lies one of the best-preserved windmills on the island. Inside it are the remains of a staircase. *With care* one can clamber up these stairs for an excellent panorama over the centre of the island — worth a detour!)

The main walk heads along the left-hand fork, but leaves this path within three minutes, to make for the Tripitos Arch. Keep an eye open for a path forking off right. The entrance to it is easily missed, because it's overgrown with bushes of *Pistacia lentiscus*. (Ten metres/yards beyond the turn off you want, you will come to a clear turning to the left. If you reach this turn-off, you'll know you've overshot the mark.)

Skirt the bushes blocking your pathway and then rejoin the path, remaining with it all the way to the coast (some shoving and floundering around is called for). You pass a noticeable doorway into a garden plot on your left a minute downhill. In autumn pink-flowering heather brightens up the countryside on this descent. Edging

around the inner slopes of a small, narrow valley, we come to the plummeting coastline. More dramatic seascapes unravel for us; the island topples off into the sea.

Descending further, bear right and step over a flattened bit of fence. A goats' path takes us down the steep hillside. *Go carefully!* Shortly Tripitos is in sight: a towering lime-stone rock joined to the island by a thin arch. At least it *looks* very narrow, until you are actually crossing it. The descent is more awkward than vertiginous and, at about **1h** into the walk, we're high above the sea crossing the arch. (Don't attempt this crossing on windy days!)

Back on the main path, where we forked off for Tripitos, we now head to the right. Under the shade of olive trees we meander along the walled-in mule track shown oppo-site. Bushes of kermes oak and *Pistacia lentiscus* smother the walls. Alleys branch off all the way along, but we remain on the main path. Now and then a break in the trees gives us an uninterrupted view of Antipaxos. Only birds break the silence.

Attention is needed to find our next (obscure) turn-off, which comes up ten minutes after rejoining this mule track. First, look out for an alley that strikes off the path to the left. Some 60 metres (yards) beyond it, after heading right and rounding a corner to your left, you'll see a faint path heading straight off towards the left, following a line of tall cypress trees. Here the main path veers off to the right, soon passing an enclosed garden, but we bear left on the faint path, and re-enter clean olive groves. A wall descends in the same direction, on our right. Keep alongside the wall; a path joins us from the right. Within minutes we come into the back of Agorakatika — a small huddle of houses that appears out of nowhere.

Squeezing between a double-storied house on the right and a lilliputian one on the left, we come into a small square. Bear left off the square and exit onto a cement lane, at about **1h25min**. Now, if you wish to save Moggonissi Island for another day, just follow this pleasant country lane, via Giftika, down to the Gaios road (15 minutes downhill), and then turn right for Gaios — another six minutes along.

Moggonissi-bound, the main walk now heads off to the right, along a path off the top of this lane. A high stone wall runs alongside the path. (Ignore the path off left immediately into the lane.) Within a minute, a faint path curves off to the left, descending through a spacious olive grove. We join the main path two minutes down and continue along to the right. Keep straight along, leaving the trees, to walk past mounds of *Pistacia lentiscus* and very aromatic myrtle.

Moggonissi — a low mound of trees and maquis — gradually creeps into the landscape. A shallow turquoise-green inlet separates the island from Paxos. Pass beside a small cottage and soon exit onto a gravel driveway descending to the road below, then continue along to your right. Walking along the water's edge we look down into the limpid green sea. When the road ends, follow the path leading off it (this path leads to Picnic 1a; see photograph page 9), and circle the base of a hillock which is thickly wooded in cypress trees. Minutes on, a stone-built causeway allows us to cross the inlet (usually without getting our feet wet), as it quickly tapers to stream-size.

The taverna and pebbly cove lie a couple of minutes along to the left. To the right, both sides of the inlet offer good views of the cliff-bashing sea and Antipaxos. On the north side of the inlet, you can scale up the sea-cliffs to your right, to see the striking limestone rock formations. The precipitous and curving coastline resembles a succession of ancient Roman amphitheatres: a particularly fine spot to wind up our walk, at **1h45min**.

Return to Gaios via the road — a pretty stroll along the rocky shoreline. Give yourself 40 minutes. Or, if your legs won't carry you any further, you can take one of the *caiques* that ply between Gaios and Moggonissi.

Note: Intrepid walkers might like to venture on around to Kalchionissi Island to see the wild setting of the Ag Spyridon Chapel. Once over the causeway, keep right and remain close to the coast. Allow 20 minutes and expect scratched legs, twisted ankles, and a ruined pair of shoes … but expect to enjoy yourself as well! A short swim across the channel that separates the islands will get you to the church. Watch out for the giant-sized billy-goat that rules Kalchionissi — good luck!

A typical stone-laid mule track; this one is on the route from Tripitos to Moggonissi.

2 GAIOS • VELLIANITATIKA • STERNA BAY OVERLOOK • MAKRATIKA • AGRILAS BEACH • BOGDANATIKA • GAIOS

Distance: 7km/4.3mi; 1h50min

Grade: easy to moderate. Gentle descents and ascents, sometimes on rocky paths. *Not recommended in wet weather.*

Equipment: sturdy shoes, sunhat, suncream, long-sleeved shirt, long trousers, cardigan, rainwear, bathing suit, picnic, water

How to get there: 🚌 to Gaios or to the Vellianitatika turn-off
To return: 🚌 from Gaios

Short walks (even shorter if you start at the Vellianitatika turn-off):

1 Gaios—Vellianitatika—Sterna Bay—Vellianitatika—Gaios: 1h; easy. Follow the main walk to the Sterna Bay overlook and retrace your steps. 🚌 to and from Gaios (or the Vellianitatika turn-off).

2 Gaios—Makratika—Agrilas Beach—Makratika—Gaios: 1h15min; quite easy. Use the map to reach Makratika by road and then refer to the first paragraph on page 34: ('... in Makratika. Head through the archway ...'). 🚌 to and from Gaios (or the Vellianitatika turn-off).

Here's a splendid walk to whet your appetite — an *apéritif.* Crossing the island (which is only 3km across at its widest point) from east to west, you sample the rural charm of Paxos. Then, once out of the cloak of olive groves, superb sea views greet you.

Picnic 2a: This wonderful outlook over Sterna Bay is reached 15-20 minutes from Vellianitatika. Unfortunately, this splendid beach is only accessible by boat. But Agrilas Beach, the inlet on the other side of the slender spit of land north of Sterna, can be reached on foot (Picnic 2b).

Start out by using the notes for Walk 1, to reach the bar/restaurant just above the Ozias turn-off. *Pass* the bar and, in less than half a minute, climb a cement path up the hillside to Vellianitatika. (Note: This path is *not* the one just behind the restaurant, which is followed in Walk 1.) A good minute uphill, pass through a junction (bearing right) and join a driveway which exits onto a cement lane alongside the village church. Continue past the church. Derelict buildings, and houses partially obscured in plant-crammed gardens, sit back in the trees. Notice how tall these olive trees are. Some attain a height of 15 metres (50 feet), and they can live for up to 1500 years!

Five minutes beyond the church we fork off this lane onto a stony track that strikes off to the right. Cypresses pierce the silvery-green mantle of the olive trees. Pass by another, smaller church, and come to a fork. Keep left. Clumps of red-berried *Pistacia lentiscus* now become noticeable. The resin from this shrub is supposed to preserve the gums — and cure toothache as well.

Ten minutes from Vellianitatika the track comes to an end. Follow the path flanked by stone walls that leads straight off it. Garden plots hide behind the walls. A lean grove of cypress trees provides a brief interlude before we exit into the maquis and garigue — an impenetrable blanket of low bushy (and often thorny) scrub. On Paxos this consists chiefly of spiny broom (*Calicotome villosa*), Spanish broom (*Spartium junceum*), *Pistacia lentiscus*, myrtle, Mediterrranean buckthorn, and kermes oak.

A minute out of the trees the stupendous cliff-top lookout over Sterna Bay (Picnic 2a) shown opposite awaits you. Not too close to the edge! You look across a succession of sweeping bays bound by towering cliffs. Valleys slice back off them, leaving narrow inlets in their wake. Far below us lies a white stony beach that dips into a pale blue sea. Unfortunately, this enticing beach is only accessible by boat. The path quickly fades out as it descends along the edge of the cliff. Go with care. Low bushy juniper shrubs dot the sea-slope and, with luck, you may spot a few swallow-tail butterflies.

When you're ready to leave this exhilarating spot, return to Vellianitatika and follow the lane back towards Gaios. Two minutes beyond Vellianitatika, off the lower side of a sharp curve to the right (the beginning of an S-bend), you'll see an alley descending off to the left through houses. Take it. It exits onto the main road just below our next turning-off point, which is the charming little Venetian church of Il Conde (also called 'Panto-kratoras') in Makratika. Head through the archway of the impressive campanile. The last of the Venetian mayors had a doorway specially built to enable him to enter the church on his horse.

Continuing along, we cross a track and pick up a fainter track, which soon narrows into a path. It will lead us down to Agrilas Beach (Picnic 2b). Descending amidst a mass of stone wall terracing, we come upon the curious buildings shown below: one of them resembles a shrine, the other is a conical construction. Below these two sits another which houses a well. Here our route bears left briefly, before it finally descends to cross the valley floor. Ignore the faint fork-off to the right. Heather, kermes oak, *Pistacia lentiscus*, and *Coronilla emerus* (Scorpian senna, which has clusters of brilliant yellow flowers in spring) hedge in the path.

Some **1h** en route (15 minutes from Makratika) we jump down onto this secluded stony cove — one of the few accessible swimming places on the west coast of the island. The bladed crest of the rocky promontory on our left (the spit of land you can see in the photograph on page 32) offers us another fine angle of Sterna Bay.

Limonium bellififolium, Crithmum maritimum (rock samphire, a fleshy, pale yellow-flowering plant, once widely collected in Britain for pickling), and *Anthyllis hermanniae* (a small spiny shrub that has bright yellow flowers in spring) sprout between the rocks.

Refreshed and home-ward bound, make for Makratika: straight off the beach keep right and up-hill; a minute later, go left at the fork. Back at the village, follow the road up to your left and, at the Gaios junction in Bog-danatika (less than 10 minutes uphill), descend to Gaios, now only 15 minutes away.

On our way to Agrilas Beach, we come upon some curious stone buildings below Makratika.

3 GAIOS • GEROMONACHES • FONTANA • KANGATIKA • LOGGOS

Distance: 5.5km/3.5mi; 1h20min   **More photos pages 10, 15, 19, 43**

Grade: fairly strenuous ascent at the start of the walk; otherwise easy. The beginning of the walk is *not recommended in wet weather* (when you could substitute Short walk 2 below).

Equipment: sturdy shoes, sunhat, suncream, long-sleeved shirt, long trousers, cardigan, rainwear, bathing suit, picnic, water

How to get there: 🚐 to Gaios
To return: 🚐 from Loggos

Short walks:

1 Gaios—Geromonaches—Fontana: 50min; grade as above. Return by 🚐 from Fontana.

2 Fontana—Kangatika—Loggos: 30min; easy. 🚐 to Fontana and return from Loggos.

3 Loggos—Koutsi—Marmari Beach—Loggos: 35min; moderate to strenuous, with a very steep ascent at the beginning and some scrambling on the paths between the beaches. Take the Lakka road out of Loggos and climb the first steep lane cutting off to the left beyond Loggos. Keep right all the way up and, in five minutes, reach a tightly-bunched hamlet. Ascend the steps and pass through the houses, bearing neither right nor left. Meet a track on the other side of the hamlet and follow it. In a minute you head through a confusion of tracks at an intersection: keep to the main, middle, track. Approaching the trunk of the derelict windmill shown on page 19, come to a fork. Take the branch to the left, which takes you through Koutsi and out onto the main road. Turn right and, a minute uphill, turn off left down a cement lane. Three minutes along keep straight on through a junction, cross a crest, and descend past Villa Chryssa. From here, refer to the last paragraph on page 42 (Walk 4): you have a choice of routes back to Loggos, and you can explore the pretty coastline and its many coves. 🚐 to and from Loggos.

C limbing into the hills that look out over the harbour at Gaios, we stumble upon the abandoned and enchanting hamlet of Geromonaches. Sitting here amidst the sagging walls and derelict buildings, time really does stand still. Continuing on, we traipse over the island's backbone of hills. Rustic villages dot the countryside; these too echo abandonment, with their shuttered villas and forgotten gardens ... idyllic spots for day-dreaming.

To start the walk, leave the Gaios bus station and follow for a few moments the road forking right to Bogdanatika (see plan of Gaios on page 6). Some metres (yards) along, turn off right onto a gravel track, soon passing a church. Immediately beyond the church, take the track striking off to the left. It appears to end half a minute uphill but, in fact, it simply narrows, squeezing past a grand but rather dilapidated flight of steps which mount a water cistern. You exit onto the wide gravel track that scars the inclines above Gaios. Bear right along this track.

From a corner, some three minutes along, we have a tremendous view over this very photogenic fishing port (see page 15) — and the pine studded island of St Nicholas. Here we leave the track, just as it curves round to the left: we head left up a steep rocky path. Pass two houses on your left a minute uphill. The tall stems of autumn-flowering sea-squill fleck the terraced inclines. Ignore side paths; keep right and uphill. As you climb, the bay unravels into a stunning sight, with its blends of greens and blues from the vegetation and the sea. Boats dot the inlet, which looks more like a river where it curls around St Nicholas. You spot, too, some remnants of the islet's Venetian fortress (1423), its ramparts swallowed up amidst the island's tangle of shrubs and trees.

The smaller island beyond St Nicholas, Panagia (seen in the photograph on page 10), is the setting for a nunnery and church bearing the same name. The 17th-century church occupies the site of an earlier Christian church; its decorations are said to be the finest of any church on Paxos. The saint's day, 14th August, is celebrated with a procession to Moni Panagias.

Spent shotgun cartridges littering the ground testify to the wealth of birds in this area. Soon a valley slides away below us and, at around **15min** from Gaios, we come out onto a farm track. Metres (yards) uphill to our left, we veer right off this track, following another track back into the trees. A couple of minutes along, the track ends. Paths fork

off both left and right. A shrine (which looks rather like a public WC) stands inside the left-hand fork. Geromonaches is still in hiding at this point. Head up to the left, and the hamlet soon discloses itself.

Derelict buildings line the solid, but now crumbling walls beside the mule track. And peering into every doorway and over every wall in this abandoned hamlet is what makes this walk such fun. Four olive presses lie amongst the ruins. You'll also see an enormous *sterna* (water deposit) off the pathway to your right. This village (Picnic 3; see photograph on the next page) is one of my favourite spots on Paxos, and I hope you enjoy it as much as I do.

When the path forks (at the other end of the hamlet) bear left uphill. A minute up, the way veers across the hill to the right, and the path fades. We briefly follow a terrace wall on our left, then swing uphill back between walls again. Back on the track, less than five minutes uphill, turn right along it. Pass a few dwellings nestled back in the trees and the tracks that turn off down to them. On the top of the crest, small outcrops of limestone are a dominant feature of the landscape. You have a panorama across the eastern flank of Paxos to the tail of Corfu, and over to Epirus.

When you reach the road (close on **30min** from Gaios), head left. In two minutes meet a junction in Bogdanatika. Bear right, following the Loggos road. The prominent campanile of Agios Charalambos, thrusting up through

cypress trees on the hillside ahead, serves as a landmark in the surrounding countryside.

A minute above the Vlachopoulatika turn-off, at a sharp corner, we fork right onto a small track. The inclines are cloaked in a thicket of greenery, with trees and bushes vying for space. Our way quickly narrows into a rough goats' path, and we look down into a densely-wooded valley below. Mind the path here; it's a menace of jutting lumps of rock. Ignore paths descending to the

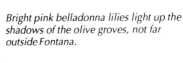

Bright pink belladonna lilies light up the shadows of the olive groves, not far outside Fontana.

right, but *do* watch out for the small patches of kermes oak tearing at your legs.

Re-entering olive groves, we soon drop down onto a farm track. Turning up to the left, pass below a small clump of hillside houses. (Note: If you are doing this walk in reverse, this obscure turn-off lies 100 paces below the village parking area and 17 paces *before* a stone wall below the track on your left.)

We now wind in and out of the steep hillsides under the shade of olive trees. On Paxos and Corfu the olives are left to fall from the trees. You'll often see netting overhead, above the mule tracks. It's tied between the trees to catch the olives as they fall. In the Mediterranean and the rest of Greece, the trees are generally beaten to make the olives fall.

Some **50min** en route, come onto a wide gravel road and enter Fontana. Keep straight on through the village centre. This scattered settlement boasts three churches and three bars. Rejoining the Loggos road, head along it to the right. Five minutes further on, leave the road and climb the first cement lane mounting the ridge above you (on your left). A short strenuous ascent brings you to a number of houses set back unnoticed on a shaded hilltop. Minutes uphill, now on gravel, see a path heading straight off the

Spare the time for delightful old abandonded hamlets like Geromonaches, shown here — one of my favourite spots on Paxos (Picnic 3).

track to the right (off a sharp curve to the left). Follow the path and in two minutes descend into the hamlet of Zernatika, where you meet a cement lane.

Continuing to the left, we now branch off the lane as it swings down to the right, and we round the hillside. These lanes make for some superb rambling. Outside the summer months, moss cushions the ground and clings to the trunks of the trees. Old villas rest in silent neglect off the side of the track. Three minutes along, the track ends, outside the gateway to a storybook garden, lush with trees and shrubs. The cottage enveloped by the garden is licked by the filtering rays of sunlight. Here steps lead us down onto yet another lane just below.

Cyclamen

Euphorbia dendroides (Tree spurge)

Bear left on this new lane and pass through a sprinkling of houses and, further on, pass by a church. The remains of a windmill can be seen through the trees, crowning the top of a crest below. (Short walk 3 would take you past this windmill; see photograph page 19.) Windmills — used for the grinding of corn, maize and barley — were once a noticeable feature of the island's landscape; there were some 16 of them. Now, unfortunately, only the shells of these mills remain, thanks to the vandalism of the occupying forces during World War II. Walk 1 passes nearby one of the best-preserved windmills on Paxos.

Vitex agnus-castus (Chaste tree)

Senecio

Dropping down the flank of a valley, the lane grows steeper — put on the brakes! It twists and winds all the way down to the valley floor, where we meet the Lakka—Loggos road. Loggos lies a couple of minutes along to your right. Time for a cool beer, and there is no better place to have it than looking out over this exquisite little bay, shown on pages 4-5 and 43.

Juniperus oxycedrus (Juniper)

4 GAIOS • KAKI LAGADA BEACH • FONTANA • KIPIADI BEACH • LOGGOS

Distance: 6km/3.7mi; 1h20min   **See also photographs pages 4-5, 43**

Grade: moderate to strenuous for less experienced walkers, quite easy for fit ramblers. A couple of short but steep ascents midway. *Not recommended in wet weather.*

Equipment: sturdy shoes, sunhat, suncream, long-sleeved shirt, long trousers, cardigan, rainwear, bathing suit, picnic, water

How to get there: 🚌 to Gaios
To return: 🚌 from Loggos

Alternative walk and Short walks:

1 Gaios—Fontana—Kipiadi Beach—Fontana: 1h15min; grade as above. This walk makes a lovely beach day. Follow the main walk to Kipiadi; then retrace the same route. 🚌 from Fontana to return.

2 Fontana—Kipiadi Beach—Loggos: 40min and easier than Alternative walk 1 above. Pick up the main walk at Fontana and carry on to Loggos. 🚌 to Fontana and return 🚌 from Loggos.

3 Loggos—Levrechio Beach—Marmari Beach—Kipos Beach and return: 30min; easy, but along roughish paths. Use the map to reach these beaches; the route is straightforward. 🚌 to and from Loggos.

This hike takes us to the picturesque fishing village of Loggos, shown on pages 4-5 and 43. Following the coastline, we dip down into enticing little coves, sampling them as we go, and climb out again, weaving our way through thickets of cypress trees.

To start the walk, we leave Gaios on the New Port road, watching the early morning boats depart along this pretty stretch of waterway. Just over **15min** out of Gaios, turn off the main road (no longer sealed) as it veers inland for Bogdanatika: take a rough gravel road branching off down to the right. A tangle of scrub and trees covers the sea-slopes. Epirus lies over to our right, and up ahead the bright limestone cliffs of Cape Asprokavos (the setting for Walk 20 in *Landscapes of Corfu*) glare across at us. Small inviting coves just below the road give us a taste of what's to come.

A further ten minutes along, having already circled behind Kaki Lagada Beach (the third cove you pass) you reach the path down to it and turn right. Everyone

We approach Kipiadi via a little wood of cypress trees. This bright-white beach lights up the entire landscape.

seems to pass by this quiet beach. A large solitary house enclosed by a fence sits above you. To continue the walk, take the path that heads up alongside the fence. Three minutes up, the way becomes overgrown, but a well-worn detour lets you pass through a hole in the fence and onto a cement drive. Actually, you are trespassing: this property surrounds a holiday villa, so go quickly and quietly to continue up the drive. A couple of minutes up you can exit through another convenient hole, by the gate, and remain on the lane. (Note: Should this fence be repaired, and you are unable to plough through the scrub blocking the path either, return to the road and climb to Fontana, where you can pick up the walk again by referring to the map. Allow an extra 20 minutes if you take the road.)

A steep climb now takes you up through tall dark green spires of cypress. Bear left at the T-junction five minutes up. Entering cool olive groves, the way eases out. Ignore the track joining from the left. On the outskirts of Fontana (just over **40min** en route) encounter a small track forking off right. Head along it. Colourful gardens and orchards enhance the rustic appeal of this pleasant farming settlement. Curious onlookers will invariably inquire 'Pooh pas?' — the intonation making it abundantly clear that you *must* be lost.

On reaching another cement lane, some three minutes along, turn right towards the small church, where the lane

then veers right into a knot of houses. Follow it and continue along the alley heading off it. Pass two alleys branching off right and then, at a third alley (a junction), turn down right and descend through the terracing. Two minutes below the houses a path joins you from the left. Nearer the sea the way becomes clearer. We brush up against mastic shrubs and then enter a small cypress wood. When you meet a fork, bear left and descend alongside a walled-in olive grove.

(If you feel like doing some exploring, the right-hand fork takes you down a fairly rough path to Alati Beach, some seven minutes away. The magnificent backdrop of cypress-forested hills makes this beach one of the most scenic spots along this stretch of the coast.)

Stepping down through the little wood we catch glimpses of marble-white Kipiadi Beach, shown on page 41. Close on **1h** into the walk we're on this fair-sized beach. It's only now that we notice the big blobs of oil and the plastic containers that litter it. But its 'undiscovered' appeal soon overrides all that ... or at least until the sailing schools arrive.

When you've had your fill of solitude, head up into the low-slung valley that opens back off the beach. About three minutes along from where you came down onto the beach, a well-trodden path reveals itself cutting up through the bushes. (Note: If you are doing the walk from Loggos, pick up your continuation to Fontana just beyond what appears to be a rocky streambed which empties out into the sea.) You're soon swallowed up amidst the cypresses again. Pass through a crumbled stone wall and then an old broken fence. Ignore the path striking off right three minutes uphill.

This gentle climb brings you up to a staggered junction a minute along: first keep left, and then go right — always straight up. Coming to houses, reach a drive and follow it to the right. A minute later, go right again, along a cement lane. Crossing a crest, the way drops down to the left, passing Villa Chryssa.* Turn off some 60 metres (yards) below this villa, down a path forking off left alongside a hedge of tall cypresses. You descend into a cool thicket of trees and bushes. Soon a path joins you from the left, just after you've gone down some steps. (Some 30 paces beyond this point, a path branching off to the right, up steps and alongside a garden wall, leads to Marmari Beach within two minutes.)

*See note opposite

Accommodation on Paxos is chiefly in villas. Some are extremely luxurious and in secluded surroundings; others, like bright-white 'Marika' here at the port in Loggos afford a taste of Greek life right in the heart of a small community. (Taken from Bar ΕϑΡΘΝΗ; see below.)

Heading through a junction, keep right for the last beach en route — Levrechio. This one is smaller and more popular than the others on our itinerary, because Loggos lies just around the corner, in the next bay. A few modest tourist villas overlook this stony beach.

To make for Loggos, take the cement lane out and descend to the right when you meet the road. A couple of minutes down you're in the friendly seaside village. Bar ΕϑΡΘΝΗ is the perfect place to put your feet up — you won't find a friendlier bar anywhere.

*At this point (as you are passing Villa Chryssa), a detour (which will only cost you a few extra minutes, plus a few ups and downs) can be taken. It introduces two more tourist-brochure coves. Explorers who wish to make the detour should continue down the lane. When it forks, bear right, to pass Villa Kypos, where the lane ends. From here a path steps its way down to Kipos Beach (Picnic 4), less than five minutes from Villa Chryssa. Then return to the fork and take the other turning: a wide cement path takes you past two houses and then continues as a dirt path zig-zagging down the hillside to Marmari Beach, three minutes down. (Note: If a fence has been built here to prevent your descent to Marmari, there is another path down to this beach further along the route of the main walk.) At the end of Marmari Beach you can pick up a path that will take you over to Levrechio Beach: Metres up the side of the bank, clamber through a gap in a stone wall on your left. Climbing amidst terracing, you exit over the same wall a minute later and, edging around the top of the bank, you descend to the sea, where another wall lets you out and down to Levrechio Beach, where you rejoin the main walk.

5 BOGDANATIKA • VLACHOPOULATIKA • AGIOI APOSTOLI CHURCH • MAGAZIA • MILOS • IPAPANTI CHURCH • LAKKA

Distance: 9.5km/6mi; 2h   **See also photographs pages 16, 20, 22**

Grade: fairly easy, but quite long. The detour to Erimitis Bay (*not* part of the main walk) is tough going, overgrown in places, and steep — only recommended for fit and experienced walkers.

Equipment: sturdy shoes (or walking boots, if you're doing the detour to Erimitis Bay), sunhat, suncream, long-sleeved shirt, long trousers, cardigan, rainwear, bathing suit, picnic, water

How to get there: 🚐 to Bogdanatika
To return: 🚐 from Lakka

Short walks:

1 Bogdanatika—Vlachopoulatika—Agioi Apostoli—Magazia: 1h; fairly easy. Follow main walk to Magazia; 🚐 from Magazia to return.

2 Magazia—Milos—Ipapanti—Lakka: 1h; easy. Follow main walk from Magazia. 🚐 to Magazia to start out; 🚐 from Lakka to return.

Here's a walk *without beaches!* It's a real countryside ramble — most of it spent wandering through rustic villages deep amidst the olive groves. But a walk without sea *views* would be virtually impossible on this tiny island, and this walk has perhaps the most dramatic sea views you'll see on Paxos.

Get off the bus in Bogdanatika, at the Vlachopoulatika junction. You'll spot a bar below the road, on your left. A track sidles past the right-hand side of the bar, passing under a trellis. **We set off** along this track and head into olive groves strewn with weary old stone walls. Three minutes downhill, keep right at a fork. A minute later our track comes to an end outside a grand villa. Now take the path running along the right-hand side of the villa. At a junction, continue to the right. Gardens hidden behind forbidding walls sit back off this meandering pathway. You pass a fork-off to the right ... and perhaps get the feeling that you are walking in circles.

Some five minutes off the track a final junction requires a turn to the left. This brings us out onto a lane, along which we bear right, to join the small road into Vlacho-poulatika. The heart of the village lies just along to your left. Go and have a look at this pretty settlement. Then, continuing on, head right and descend the first turn-off on the left, to join a wide gravel road that climbs to the main road after some ten minutes. From here we overlook a deep 'V'-shaped valley cloaked in olive groves and cypress trees, and we pass a couple of farm tracks branching off to the left.

Two minutes down the main road, we turn off left onto

a narrow cement lane signposted in English to 'St Apostle Church'. Soon we enjoy a brief view of sea cliffs far below. Just ten minutes downhill, we strike off right onto a track heading between a garage and a house — another sign for the church alerts us to this turn-off.

The church stands beyond some steps at the end of this drive, **35min** into the walk. Agioi Apostoli itself is nothing special, but it is stunningly sited to take advantage of the magnificent vista over the Erimitis Cliffs, where the coastline rears up out of the azure sea into sheer chalky-coloured walls. In the churchyard a table and benches shaded by cypress trees offer an ideal picnic spot (Picnic 5). You can spend hours here contemplating the tremendous view shown on page 22.

The adventurers among you may wish to venture down to Erimitis Bay far below. There's no beach there, so that swimming (provided that the sea is *dead calm*) is from the rocks. To get there: Head along the track (below the church steps) for approximately 75 metres (yards) and, immediately after passing the colourful house below the track (on the left), descend the steps that brush alongside its garden wall. Within a minute downhill, meet a faint fork and swing right, soon crossing a dip in the hillside.

Achai Bay, not far below the setting for Picnic 5: to reach this viewpoint over the three caves in the cliffs, follow the notes on page 46, second paragraph.

Fallen olive tree branches may need skirting. Two minutes further on, a path joins from the right, and faint arrows confirm your way. Stretches of the route are a little overgrown, and you'll have to scramble over crumbled stone walls. *Don't continue if the way beomes unclear to you:* this would be too dangerous, and you are far from help. Less than ten minutes down, pass a fork off to the right (you can ascend this mule track to Magazia, on your return). Five minutes further on, or 15 minutes down from the church, standing on a water cistern overlooking the bay, you reach the end of the scramble. *Attention: The descent to the rocks below you requires great care!*

When you are ready to return, climb to the first fork off to the left and ascend to Magazia this way. An old (and, for the first three minutes, overgrown) mule track climbs steeply up into cypresses and then to the olive fields above. Some seven minutes up from the turn-off, pass a fork off to the right and a minute later another to the left; ignore them both and keep straight on. Not far below Magazia, on meeting a faint fork, head up to the left, following the remains of the mule track. A minute up, veer right. Soon exit onto the main road in Magazia. The village shop lies just up ahead on the left, if you need to 'refuel'.

The main walk does not visit Erimitis Bay. Instead, we leave the church and go back to the turn-off (two minutes back). But, before climbing back up the lane, we descend to the right and take the track following the coastline. At the end of this track, a few minutes down, we have a magnificent view back into Achai Bay. A small sandy cove (only accessible by sea) nestles in the foot of a half-moon of cliffs. If you head a short way down the path that leads off the track, you can see the three cloistered caves opening out of the sea cliffs shown in the photograph on page 45.

Return to the main road (in Magazia) and bear left, passing a shop a couple of minutes along. Three minutes beyond the shop we leave the road, turning off onto a cement lane branching off left to Manessatika (a school building stands beside the turn-off). Pass a lane off to the left. Now strolling along, just soak up the peacefulness of this silvestran countryside, the stillness broken only by the bray of a donkey calling out to anyone who will listen.

A little over five minutes off the road, come into Manessatika, where the lane forks. Keep left and shortly pass the church, followed by a tiny shop on your right —

so tiny, that you may not even notice it. An air of abandon hangs over these hamlets — the walls are decaying, and the houses are closed up.

Another fork greets us above the hamlet of Milos, some **1h15min** en route. Our way is to the right but, before heading off, continue down to the left for a few minutes, until you are near the cliff-tops. Concealed from the track, but only metres off it, is a viewpoint from where you look down into a small and narrow inlet, which is most impressive for the sheer height of its formidable walls. Then return to the fork and continue to the right.

When the way comes to an end about half a minute downhill, follow the path striking off up to the right. Almost immediately it turns back to the left, descends through houses, and then heads down the terraced hill-side. In a few minutes you step down onto a lane. Bear right along it. Five minutes later, climb to a lane cutting across in front of you.

This cool, shady lane twists and winds down into the valley: turn left downhill. You pass a private track off to the right and then, a further seven minutes along — not long after passing above Grammatikeika (the towering belfry of Ipapanti church gives away the presence of this hamlet) — you reach the turn-off into the settlement; it's the first cement lane branching off left. A couple of minutes brings you to the foot of the belfry shown here (see also Walk 7 and the photograph on page 16).

Return to the lane and continue back down into the valley floor, passing two more forks off to the left. Then join the Lakka road (really a rough track) and head left for Lakka, less than ten minutes along. A view of Lakka (but taken on the route of Walk 7) is on page 20.

The elegant campanile of Ipapanti Church, visited in both Walk 5 and Walk 7.

6 LOGGOS TO LAKKA (VIA THE COAST)

Distance: 5km/3mi; 1h10min   **See also photos pages 4-5, 20, 43**

Grade: moderate to strenuous, with plenty of ups and downs. Recommended only for fit walkers and *not recommended in wet weather*.

Equipment: sturdy shoes or walking boots, sunhat, suncream, long-sleeved shirt, long trousers, cardigan, rainwear, bathing suit, picnic, water

How to get there: 🚌 to Loggos
To return: 🚌 from Lakka

Short walks:

1   Loggos to the first two beaches and return: 50min; moderate, with steep ascents and descents. *Not recommended for young children, and dangerous in wet conditions.* These beautiful beaches are only accessible on foot or by sea. 🚌 to and from Loggos.

2   Explore the eastern arm of Lakka Bay: 30min; moderate. *Recommended for experienced walkers with a head for heights.* The path is a little rough in places, but fun. 🚌 to and from Lakka. Start out by following the promenade along the waterfront. Two minutes out, pass behind a school building. Begin your ascent on a path climbing the hillside above the school. On reaching the edge of the cliff, head up to the right and pass behind what appears to be a harbour lookout post. The path continues past a tiny cottage before edging around the cliffs. Fortunately the path is fenced in. Less than ten minutes from Lakka, the path drops down onto the seashore rocks, and here you will have to scramble on all fours — *slowly and carefully.* Floundering over the rock, bear right. Three minutes along, you will reach the end of this limestone shelf and come to a minuscule cove, the best spot from which to swim. From here scale the side of the bank above you, where the going is quite vertiginous. Tunnelling your way through scrub, you briefly follow a streambed (dry in summer). Ignore a faint fork off left a minute up. A few minutes along the streambed, climb up onto the side of the bank on your left and head alongside the streambed. Meet a junction with a water pipe crossing it; then bear right. Soon enter an olive grove. Head up the left-hand side of it and exit onto a track, at a junction. Head right here, and then go left at the next junction. From here you quickly descend back into Lakka.

T he idyllic little coves that lie scattered along the east coast make this island the gem that it is. They warrant a cove crawl, and this hike is the second half of it (the first half being Walk 4). By boat it will cost you much less energy; by foot you pay with a couple of hours and possibly a blister, but the reward certainly outshines the discomfort. Don't forget your suncream!

Begin the walk behind the old soap factory — the building with the tall chimney, on the left-hand side of the port (as you face the sea). Turn off into a driveway forking off right, beside Lola Cottage. The drive leads onto a cobbled path which climbs up behind the factory furnace. A minute uphill, branch off onto a cement path veering off to the right. Solid stone walls line your way.

Picnic 6: Climb the promontory above Loggos for this superb view of the limestone shelves collaring the coastline.

In three minutes we come to the foot of a derelict windmill that crowns the promontory hilltop (Picnic 6). From here you have the excellent view over Loggos shown on page 4. The pastel-coloured village stands just on the waterfront; olive-clad hills cascade down around it. It's picture-postcard perfect. If you climb the old mill walls for your view, *do so with the utmost care.*

Continuing on, now swing left, following the garden wall you have been circling (on your left). (A path off to the right here descends steeply to a tiny cove, three minutes below.) Barely a minute further along, you enjoy the uninterrupted view along the coastline seen in the photograph above, with its striking colour contrasts of dark green inclines, limestone-grey shoreline, and royal blue sea. The limestone shelf can be reached via a path off to the right here.

Further along the wall, you'll see the remains of a second windmill on your left. The belfry piercing the cape of olive trees, over on the right, is our immediate target. We soon pass a narrow alleyway forking off to the left. (You might like to return to Loggos this way, if you're doing Short walk 1). Keeping straight up, we reach a lane on the outskirts of Dendiatika in two minutes. Turning right, we head towards the church.

About 65 metres (yards) up, a side-track descends to your right. Follow it. When it ends, bear left along a path around the hillside. A couple of minutes on, immediately beyond a walled-in olive grove, the path drops down the steep hillside, as does the wall. *Take care* on the descent, the way is stony and slippery. Zig-zag down through the terracing, shoving your way past bushes of myrtle and mastic, and exit onto a lovely quiet 'double' cove (just over **15min** from Loggos). To reach the second half of the cove you sometimes need to scramble up and over a short stretch of bank. Here the branches of the olive trees reach out over the stony beach.

The next stretch of the walk, over to Monadentri Beach, might pose a problem. As more of the seaside land is being

bought up for development, it's being fenced off: villa owners don't like walkers on their property. At present, there is a coastal path over to the next cove, some five minutes away. Should this piece of the route ever be fenced off, the map indicates a rough fishermen's path that you can use instead. Allow an extra ten minutes (*my* time, remember!).

Agave
americana
(Century plant)

Continuing to Monadentri along the coastal path, climb (on all fours) the rocky side of the bank and follow the path that heads through the small olive grove just above. (Don't climb towards the house.) In a couple of minutes, clamber over a stone wall and flounder through scrub to the cove below. Another blissful spot, but *do* watch out for sea urchins here, amongst the stones quite close to the shore.

Cooled-off and ready for another breath-consuming ascent, find a clear path midway along the beach, which climbs a bank and disappears into a sea of heather: this path, shown on page 52, is a beautiful sight in autumn, when the hillside is a mass of pink flowers. Immediately through the wall, the way forks. Keep right. You ascend into an overgrown olive grove punctuated with cypress trees. The way begins very clearly but, some four minutes uphill — after passing a faint fork to the left — the path swings across the hillside to the right and becomes less distinct. Following it, we head up into the 'V' of a narrow gulley on our right. Two minutes futher on, we cross the dry streambed and continue up alongside it. In late September the inclines are awash with resplendent yellow *Sternbergia* (see opposite).

Approaching Apergatika, the valley fans out. Keep straight on up to the houses ahead, head over to the right below them, and then swing up to the left (the path vanishes here) — to a track barely a minute up. Turn right on the track and, some metres (yards) along, join a cement lane, where you continue northwards (right). (If you are doing the walk in the reverse direction, locate the path turn-off some 18 metres (yards) down the track that branches off the cement lane.)

Left: Sternbergia lights up the shady path we follow between Monadentri Beach and the hamlet of Apergatika.

After your visit to Monadentri cove, cooled off and ready for another breath-consuming ascent, find a clear path midway along the beach, which climbs a bank and disappears into a sea of heather: a beautiful sight in autumn, when the hillside is a mass of pink flowers.

Passing through this rustic, sleepy scattering of dwellings, we keep straight along, ignoring the fork-off to the right. In three minutes we descend to a T-junction. Bearing right, we soon meet a fork and here make a left turn down a very rough track. It steepens considerably — you virtually slide down the hillside into the most magnificent tiny cove — Lakkos. Possibly you will have this cove (**45min**) all to yourself. It's set in a slight 'dent' in the coastline, in the shadows of a darkly wooded hillside.

To return, follow the lane back uphill and keep straight on at the T-junction. (There is a short-cut uphill as well, but it is really rough going.) Ignore the confusion of tracks off to the right. Winding through the trees, we soak up the farmyard atmosphere of our surroundings. At the next junction, five minutes on, head around to the right.

But … if you haven't tired of beaches (and all the ups and downs), I can take you to yet another cove — one certain to elicit some 'oooh's and 'aaah's. This one *has* seen some development, however. Add 20 minutes to your walking time, and off you go: Some 75 metres (yards) from the last junction, where the cement begins, you see the remains of a sunken pathway cutting down the hillside on your right. It's no longer used. However, our detour, a faint path at this point, begins by crossing the top of it and dipping into the valley below. Soon the way becomes quite clear. For the first few minutes you're on the left bank, and then you cross the streambed — a real stream this time — and head along the valley floor. I think this is the prettiest pathway on Paxos; when alight with spring or autumn flowers, it looks like an illustration for a book of fairytales. Just before exiting onto Orkos Beach (seven minutes downhill), you pass to the right of an enclosure with a number of rondavels in it.

The main walk continues to Lakka, rounding the right-hand bend in the lane. Soon we catch a glimpse of the transparent green bay, through a canopy of trees. It's one of the island's prize beauty spots. (The photograph on page 20 shows this setting from the path of Walk 7 — a promontory to the northwest of Lakka.) Less than ten minutes along, the lane curves sharply to the left, bringing us down to a fork. (Ignore the track branching off to the right just beforehand.) Taking the left-hand fork, we pass some cottages. The way then swings back to the left as it drops down into Lakka, which is just below. At **1h10min** (1h30min for those of us who included the detour to Orkos Beach), it's time to plonk ourselves down at a bar with the sea lapping at our side.

Some other flowers you might see on Paxos (from left to right): Ranunculus, Anemone, Anacamptis pyramidalis (Pyramidal orchid), and Urginea maritima (Sea squill).

7 LAKKA • AKR LAKKA • VASSILATIKA • IPAPANTI CHURCH • LAKKA

Distance: 7.5km/4.5mi; 1h50min   See also photos pages 16, 20, 47

Grade: moderate to strenuous for less experienced walkers, with some (short) rough stretches en route. The detour to the 'fishermen's perch' is only recommended for the experienced walker, because of the possibility of vertigo. In wet weather, don't venture off the tracks and lanes.

Equipment: sturdy shoes or walking boots, sunhat, suncream, long-sleeved shirt, long trousers, cardigan, rainwear, bathing suit, picnic, water

How to get there: 🚐 to Lakka
To return: 🚐 from Lakka

Short walks:

1   Around Cape (Akr) Lakka: 1h; easy, but involves some scrambling through hillside scrub and a few short ascents and descents. Follow the main walk up to where you reach the cement lane swinging round in front of you (at 40min). Here bear left and descend to Lakka, remaining on the lane. Take care around the 'rock tables' near Plani Beach, where the path is in danger of crumbling away.

2   Lakka—Aronatika—Lakka: 1h20min; fairly easy. Follow the main walk (excluding the detour to the 'fishermen's perch') to the junction of tracks at just over the 50min-mark. Here descend a lane to the left, which forks immediately. Take the left fork and head down a steep gravel track. In two minutes, pass a solitary church. A minute later, outside a gateway, when the track ends, continue along the path that carries on, passing below a house with a garden. Follow the streambed briefly, before crossing it in two minutes. The remains of a cobbled way lead you up the hillside, above what appears to be a derelict village. Rounding the nose of the ridge, you pass above a couple of occupied houses and, less than a minute later, meet a cement lane cutting down in front of you. Descend on this lane until you reach the Manessatika lane (three minutes downhill); here bear left and join a gravel road. Head left for Lakka.

Explore Cape (Akr) Lakka and discover a variety of beaches and seascapes. Then move on to the plunging escarpment of the west coast, an inaccessible wall of cliffs that will leave you in awe. Inland, the countryside is a timeless masterpiece. Enchanting old lanes lead you through the Paxos of centuries ago … and the Paxos of today — there is little difference between the two.

To start the walk, we take the steps up between the last two restaurants at the western end of Lakka's port. We pass below a church and then continue around the coastline to the second and larger beach. Both of these beaches are wonderful for children.

Straight off the end of the second beach, head up into thick scrub, following a steep goats' path that climbs the face of the hill. The way forks, but both branches come out onto the crest above. From the top of the ridge you have a magnificent panorama over the beautiful crystal clear waters of the harbour. You might like to stop here for Picnic 7a, in the setting shown on page 20. Looking across the northern side of the enclosing arm, you see Corfu, from the white cliffs of the south to the hilly west coast. A few minutes along the crest, you scramble down to a small beach in the neck of the headland — the final part of the descent on all fours. The beach here is usually covered in seaweed.

A quieter and more appealing beach (another place to enjoy Picnic 7a) lies on the northern side of the headland. Returning from the neck, it's two minutes back and then the first turn-off to the right. Again we flounder through

Close on 30 minutes from Lakka, we slide down onto isolated Plani Beach, where curious rock 'tables' jut out into the sea.

scrub, in three minutes leaving the mouth of a streambed and coming upon the dazzling white-rock cove shown below. It's backed by impressive cliffs, and the water is an inviting turquoise-green — but note that the sea *can* be quite rough on this side of the point.

For the next part of our expedition, we return along the path on the top of the crest but, instead of descending back to the beaches, we keep straight on past our turn-off, go through a fence, and come to a house. (Watch out for the dog here!) We then follow a faint path veering off left and circle below the house, to join a driveway at the other end of it. (En route, we pass another path descending back down to the beach.) An intersection follows: we turn up right, towards the lighthouse.

Some 60 metres (yards) along the track, a path cutting off left takes us down to our next beach. We pass in front of a walled-in garden, before coming out into maquis. The way veers left below the lighthouse, through this leg-scratching scrub. A couple of lighthouse paths join us.

Close on **30min** from Lakka, we slide down onto isolated Plani Beach and an emerald-green bay. Around the corner to our left, curious limestone 'tables' jut out into the sea. Cliffs tower in the background. If you decide to walk around on these rock 'tables', go *carefully*; they are slippery and crumbly. You can continue around the shelf for another three minutes or so, for the beautiful view of the sea caves and cove shown on page 55.

Return to the intersection where you turned off for the lighthouse but, this time, keep straight on — until you reach a cement lane swinging round in front of you, three

Missorachi Beach, one of the settings for Picnic 7a.

minutes up (**40min**). Follow this lane up to the right. (But those of you doing Short walk 1 descend to the left here.) Wandering amidst these peaceful sylvan hills you head through Dalietatika — a shy sprinkling of cottages set back in the trees. The houses become more dispersed and the countryside 'friendlier'.

A little under ten minutes up the lane, keep an eye out for the most colourful little homestead on Paxos. The colours are perhaps not those that you or I would choose, but this is a real nursery-rhyme setting — the kind of place where you would expect to see the gingerbread man come bursting out of the front door. The cottage sits off a small lane that forks off to the left. Our gentle ascent gives us a chance to view the large open valley through which we'll head back to Lakka, before we descend to a junction (at around **50min**). At this point, those of you doing Short walk 2 descend left and left again.

Sure-footed walkers with a head for heights can now make a 'detour' (the time is *included* in the walking times below) to a lonely 'fishermen's perch' set precariously in the sea-cliffs. To get to it, continue just beyond the lane on the left and then fork off right on the path running alongside the walls of a stone-built enclosure. Keep left around the enclosure and enter a little wood of cypress trees and pines. Within three minutes come to another wall, on your right. Some 27 paces further on, spot a goats' path descending into a narrow valley cutting down to the sea, through a gap in the woods. Pushing through bushes, you drop down into a dry rocky streambed, before swinging across the steep right-hand wall of the valley, where sure-footedness and a head for heights is necessary. Stepping back down into the streambed may require scrambling on all fours — *take care!* Some ten minutes from the junction, standing at the mouth of the valley, you look down over rocky ledges (please leave these to the local fishermen) into a pounding sea. This is a spot in which to rest a while and contemplate ... as long as the wind is not howling up the valley (notice the angle of the windblown trees growing here!).

Returning to (or continuing from) the junction, we follow the lane up to the end, to the deserted village of Vassilatika. Large shuttered homes sit in forlorn neglect amongst the trees. At the end of the lane, steps climb up through a garish blue and white archway to a derelict, but still rather imposing, Venetian villa. Note the fine verandah on the upper storey.

Setting off again, head off the lane along the mule track. High walls shade the path. Soon leave the olive plots behind and emerge into a tangled mass of maquis. Some five minutes from Vassilatika you find yourself near the very edge of a very high precipice. A metre (yard) over to your right, you're looking straight down into a keyhole-shaped chasm that slices inland from the sea. What a sight! An exhilarating, but rather frightening, lookout point! *Don't venture too near the edge.* The path skirts this gaping inlet and is never far from the cliffs. A ruined windmill peers above the juniper bushes on the hilltop ahead.

Having circled the inlet we join a track (**1h20min**). Now we descend to the left. Less than five minutes down, just beyond a small cottage set behind walls, we pick up a mule track dropping off the track to the right. (It branches off before the track curves sharply left.) Descending rapidly, we zig-zag down between steeply banked terraces into a large valley below.

Shortly the impressive baroque campanile of Ipapanti Church (see page 47) catches your eye through the trees. A couple of minutes down, exit onto a path and head over to the church (on your right). The bright ochre facade of this Byzantine church (see page 16) cheers up this dark corner of the valley. Ipapanti (Picnic 7b) is the oldest church on the island and unique for its two circular rooftop domes.

Unfortunately it is kept locked. One of the only springs on the island is found in the little gulley you crossed, behind the church. It's a lush spot. The path is flooded with cyclamen in autumn. Not a sound can be heard in Grammatikeika, the village above.

Now making for Lakka, we head back out on the path, keeping straight on from where we joined it. We step down between a couple of houses a few minutes along and join a driveway just below them. This leads down to the Manessatika lane, where we head left. On meeting the Lakka road (which is more like a wide track), we bear left again for Lakka, 15 minutes away.

Distance: 7.5km/4.5mi; 1h45min

Grade: moderate, with a steady 15-minute ascent at the outset. *Not recommended in wet weather*, when the tracks get very muddy.

Equipment: sturdy shoes, sunhat, suncream, long-sleeved shirt, long trousers, cardigan, rainwear, bathing suit, picnic, water

How to get there: 🚢 During the season *caiques* run virtually non-stop from Gaios to Vrika on Antipaxos (journey time 20-30 minutes). There is also a service from Loggos and Lakka, but it is less frequent.
To return: 🚢 from Vrika; the last *caiques* leave at 17.00. Always verify the last boat back; departure times may change!

Short walks:

1 Vrika—Vigla—Voutoumi Beach—Vrika: 35min; grade as above. This walk shows you a good cross-section of the island with the minimum of effort. Use the main walk notes up to the end of page 60. Then, to continue on to Voutoumi Beach, refer to the third paragraph on page 62 ('Now we visit those irresistible sandy beaches …').

2 Vrika—Vigla—Agrapidia (port)—Stavrou—Voutoumi Beach—Vrika: 1h; grade as above. Do the main walk, but exclude the lighthouse detour, by keeping right at the intersection.

Note: the only tavernas on the island are at Vrika, but there's a bar above Voutoumi Beach.

Most holiday-makers on Paxos make a day trip to Antipaxos — word quickly gets around about the island's sandy beaches. Few people, however, venture beyond these beaches, and most tourists remain unaware

Voutoumi Bay, one of the settings for Walk 8 and Picnic 8, is considered by many to be the most beautiful beach in all of Greece.

that this speck in the sea (only 3 square kilometres!) has more to offer than sand and sea. Less than fifteen minutes uphill from Vrika (where the *caiques* land) the salubrious tangle of vineyards and garden plots shown opposite awaits you. Cobbled alleys criss-cross the island's hump like a great maze, connecting the farm dwellings that dot the landscape. Do the island justice — go out for a stroll.

Stumble out of the *caique* at the small cove of Vrika and **start the walk.** Head up the roughly bulldozed track that climbs to Vigla. A minute up, pass a wide path off to the left, which leads to another cove (Messovrika) and Voutoumi Beach — settings for Picnic 8. Within the first ten minutes, the main track forks off left for Voutoumi and the port; we, however, keep straight up. The slopes are thickly woven in the ubiquitous maquis. We have a fine view over Paxos, to Corfu and mainland Greece.

Just after passing a terraced vineyard (and a fork off to the right), the track comes to an end. Follow the pathway continuing off it. A surprise awaits you as you mount the island's 'hump' — quite a substantial settlement of vineyards and gardens covers the crest. Tired walls lean over the gardens, hiding their greenery from view. Bear left at the first junction you meet and follow the main path.

We pass by shuttered stone houses with trellised courtyards. When it's grape-picking time, the island becomes a hive of activity, and the musky odour of crushed grapes permeates the air. Face-lifted cottages (and even some new houses) suggest that the 20th century has finally arrived here on Antipaxos as well. If you're not pressed for time, do some exploring, wander up some of the many side-alleys off the main route. Looking over the vineyards below you, the turquoise blue waters off Voutoumi Beach steal your attention with their alluring brightness. This beach, one of the finest in Greece, is *the* beauty spot of Antipaxos. The hills of Epirus rise in the background.

Some five minutes off the track, we join a cemented lane to the port and pass a fork off to the right (which will return us to this lane later on in the walk). Descending on this lane, we look straight across onto the impressive northwest coast of Greece. Some 30 metres (yards) down the lane, a track branches off to the left. This will take us to Voutoumi later in the walk, on our return from the lighthouse. (Those of you doing Short walk 1 turn left here.)

Right: Looking out over vineyards, the turquoise blue waters of Voutoumi Beach steal your attention with their alluring brightness.

Some **30min** into the walk we're down in the sheltered little port of Agrapidia. A few colourful fishing boats sit moored to the pier. We now ascend the concrete lane on the other (southeastern) side of the port: a steep climb which returns us to gardens and vineyards. Notice the absence of olive trees on this island. Minutes up, the way reverts to gravel, and we reach an intersection. The walk continues to our left on an even rougher track, to the lighthouse (but Short walk 2 bears right here).

Vineyards patch the dense cloak of maquis on our approach to the lighthouse, and we see the limestone islets of Dasskalia off to our right. More of the Ionian islands lie in the distance. We reach the lighthouse after about **1h**. Circle it to the right and come to the front gate, and a pathway leading down to the pier, three minutes away. A nearby cove offers more accessible swimming: cross over the path and take the trail which cuts across a circular construction of rocks, before disappearing into the scrub. This will lead you to one of the most islolated beaches on the island — and you'll have it all to yourself.

When you've had your fill of sun and solitude, return to the intersection where you turned off for the lighthouse but, this time, head straight on into the profusion of walls and gardens. Our way quickly narrows, and we pass a track descending to the port. Back into this labyrinth of alleys, we remain on the main route. We pass a path branching off to the left, followed by one off to the right. Here our way narrows into a path. Ignore the next alley turning off to the left; continue along to the right. A minute beyond the church of Ag Emilianos, we rejoin the cement lane that we followed to descend to the port, earlier in the walk, and we turn right.

Now we visit those irresistible sandy beaches. Some 30 metres (yards) down the lane to the port, fork off left on a gravel track. Come to a fork two minutes down and go right, along the top of the crest. Keeping left at the next fork, pass a solitary WC on the side of the track and descend to a bar three minutes along (you won't be able to see it until you're almost there). This magnificently-perched bar is unrivalled on the two islands for its vista. The limpid pale blue bay and the chalk-coloured cliffs fringed with dark green vegetation create a memorable picture. A steep stairway takes you from the bar down to the beach.

Heading back from Voutoumi, seek out the path that climbs the hillside just beyond the track down to the beach. Scramble up the hillside and keep right, rounding the tops of the cliffs (don't climb straight up). You will encounter two (short) stretches of vertiginous path along here. Tunnelling through the dense vegetation, you exit down over rock onto Messovrika Beach, five minutes from Voutoumi. It's less crowded. Follow the wide path that leaves from behind the beach and, two minutes uphill, descend to Vrika.

Don't forget that the last *caique* leaves at 17.00!

Landscapes of Corfu

While you're on Paxos, why not explore some landscapes on nearby Corfu, with its still-unspoiled rural interior? There are frequent ferries (see timetables on page 7 of this book). There's also a good bus service on Corfu, if you're not renting a car. Below is a photograph taken on one of my favourite walks on Corfu: this idyllic setting is a short stroll from one of the popular hotels, but most tourists never see it! You can obtain this book from the same source as *Landscapes of Paxos*.

Landscapes of Corfu —
4 car tours • 67 long and short walks • 40 picnic suggestions
pull-out touring map • 11 large-scale full-colour walking maps
30 colour photographs • bus timetables

✿ Index

Geographical names only are included in this index; for other entries, see Contents, page 3. Page numbers in bold type indicate photographs. All entries below may be found on the pull-out map. See also brief index to photographs and drawings of some island flora on page 6.